WISEHEART

JIA APPLE

Also by Jia Apple

Oft Made to Wonder

The Tell

WISEHEART

a book of poems

JIA APPLE

AWAKEN VILLAGE

PRESS

Printed in the United States of America.

Cover and interior design by: Andrea Gibb
Author photo by: Barb Chandler

To contact the author or for permission requests,
email: jia@thepictureseer.com.

ISBN 978-1-957408-11-8 (paperback)
ISBN 978-1-957408-20-0 (ebook)

Library of Congress Control Number: 2024927600

Published by Awaken Village Press,
Sioux Falls, South Dakota, U.S.A.

www.awakenvillagepress.com

I dedicate this collection of poetry to every love
I've ever embraced.

These words are about you.

Jia

contents

acknowledgments

Thank you, Barbara Bennett, for your ongoing support and willingness to edit this work twice. Acts of God can be a real bitch.

My warm thanks go to those who have inspired each one of these poems. You know who you are, and I love you deeply.

Thank you, Mother, for your name that continues to be a significant part of who I am and has served as the perfect title for this collection.

To Amanda and the team at Awaken Village Press, I am deeply appreciative of your willingness to publish this and show it to the poetry lovers of the world.

To all whose hands have helped with the creation of this book, I thank you.

the nest

At birth
Upon her downy breast
Wanting of my mother's play
Surrendering to natural things
Knowing nothing of more
Or less
An infant

But then as often can be
Nature resists
Nurture falls to deafened ears
Stifles innocence

Until
Intended for death
Softly landing upon the earthen floor
To expose
Foe

Rejection holds no promise but to strengthen
resolve

So, I resolve
And such as it were, with broken bits, I wing a
crooked flight
To you

Soft to my touch
Taste alien to my thirst
I drink
Slaked

Your arms caress me
Whispers say
I love you

Atop this world
I see no fray, no foe
Only me
Only you

Your heart
So skillfully prepared
Nature at her best
Your breasts upon mine
This nest

heaven

When I was a child
Mom said there were gates in heaven
like the rich people have
made of pearl
streets are made of gold she said
I don't think animals go to heaven
I thought that was a shame
especially since she loved cats and birds
so much
I asked my mother
if you could have anything
in this world
anything at all
what would it be?
She said she would have
a screened-in porch
off the back of the house
I love my mom
more than I can say

her heart is good
I don't think her life
had a lot of pearls
or gold
Looking back
I bet she would have traded in
the giant pearl
and the Golden Freeway
to live her last days
at home
with Dad
her kids
a stray cat or two
looking through catalogs of covered porches

my extra heart

I wish there were a word I could magically say,
like
sorry
or I was wrong
A word that would make love last longer
than a flower
or one particular day
or anything else seemingly here
then gone away
The thing about it is
you never die in me—
this love
You stay like an extra heart
beating away the days with me
Maybe you know it, too
maybe not
It would be enough if you smiled and said
everything would be okay one day
and it really isn't so much about being in pain

and wanting relief
It feels more like being thirsty
like missing a friend's smile
Maybe the magic words are
you were right
I'm bad
guilty
can't be forgiven
but that doesn't feel right either
I believe in magic
my love will build a bridge
while I'm busy not looking
so that one day we can walk
between these hearts
and be friends again

mary and me

(A tribute to Mary Magdalene)

In our hearts
ghosts live terrible lives
looked upon by others
as unfortunate choices

They hover within
feeding on attention
growing fatter with every glance
Ghosts devouring happiness

Submission is a quiet voice
I strain to hear

No love can save me but my own
a light to extinguish apparitions' bites
Still, there are clouds within
playing shadow puppets on my hills

Mary takes my hand

So I cherish me and dance
until I can conjure a smile

Eventually, ghouls disband
none are left
save my memories
Memories that have gone
forgiven

november

November used to be about leaves
the smell of pies baking
Colors crunched under my feet as someone in
the neighborhood lit a fire
I felt safer knowing the cellar was stocked with
beets, pickles, and beans
Winter is getting cozy by the fire and can
barely keep his eyes open
long enough to smell the pies
While the old man sleeps, his clouds and ice
appear
It was a spooky play, and I loved it every year
Then I came into my own summer
It was one day in November when winter came
too soon
Sleep settled on a Spring evening when it was
least expected
November said to Spring, you are mine
And though the Spring could have burst a

thousand petals of life into that cold face
she shuddered in her youth and fell silent
for it was night
We all know of that last frost and how some
of the early buds are taken
Such was the same in this case
My summer is gone and autumn is upon me

November's colors are coming back to me now
I can almost smell the pie and the fire
My Spring was taken but only for a season
Soon enough, winter will pay me a call
November, you taunted me and filled me
You played outside the lines
Mine was not to be a fresh bud frozen in time
mine was not the Spring to bear it
Mine are the seasons
Come now
November
fill me once more

sea

Autumn lends to remembrance
these years
What fun we had in early summer
The undertow didn't have a chance
to win me over
Plenty times
I drifted out to sea
Yours was an island I found
whose beach, sandy white
and palms delighted me
Brown and wet we basked
Alas
the waters of Makapu'u
nearly had me
and we drifted apart
in its beautiful rage
Life, you are my vessel
I am your breath
Slippery as you seem

no destination disappoints
No sea succumbs
to winter's reflection
As well
nor do I

eostre

And then suddenly a dangerous woman
slipped in through my cracked window
Poised, she sat at my table
March winds moving through her
while she sits perfectly still
no stand of pines
no mountain pass
no wall of flames
or closed door can stop her
She moves untamed
this force of grace
inviting blades of grass and flower buds
moves me
She strikes the space I'm in
to confront my fears
Venomous as it seems
I need her

Hers is a royal entrance
the resurrection of ancient souls

hidden too long in their dreams
As she dances her dress flows
like the murmuration of starlings
Her hair is the same
All the while the pines lose their winter needles
I in my space
open the window wider
to bring my summer home

dawn

Black lace shadows listen to a silent sunset
Her sharp lines split the night
Conversations between shadows and darkness
until night conquers day

A sleepy blanket of dark settles on her prey
Twilight has gone, and the dawn seems a far-
off land
Weary souls rest their minds
as visions of violet fade to black

Dream entices her partner as sleep sweeps the
night
Together, they soar to meet the days before
days ahead
days that will never be

Streams of laughter
echoes of sorrow
exchange their haunting glances

The ice from someone's winter glares at
passersby
Familiar people
never seen before

Just as I know that I am
I know that I am and more
Given to insightful glimpses
ethereal blueprints

A sparkling spray of glitter white
catches the attention of my slumber
Reaching within to pull me
into the light
The far-off land draws me nearer
Enveloped in her arms
dawn breaks

your ways

I saw you cross the street today
your hair, brown and wispy
You took your time
with nothing more or less on your mind
than traffic
Our eyes met
leaving me wanting nothing more
than hearing your voice
or perhaps
touching you
I'm given to your ways
to your coming
your smile
the way you kiss me with your eyes
Do you see me loving you?
My heart finds comfort in your being
in your crossing the street
but mostly
in your ways

for mother

(sung to a gentle tune)

When it rains, my hair gets curly
when it snows, my nose gets red
when it's cold, my toes get chilly
when the wind blows, I'm in bed

I say a prayer when autumn leaves fall
I do a jig when music plays
Isn't life so very tempting
when lovely are the changing days?

When the trees embrace the roadside
when the snow drifts o'er the plain
something calls me from the inside
as the day begins to wane

Gentle are the curls that crown me
flakes of snow land on my head
warming fires tend to know me
when the wind blows, I'm in bed

another day

I felt like walking today
so I headed south
Las Cruces bound
Thoughts in my head
about the reserves
stored in my lean body

I wondered about my shoes
and if they would last
and blisters
there would be many blisters

I wondered what shin splints felt like
if I had enough water
Would I die if I drank from the Rio Grande?

The mountains are so long and high
when walking by them
Driving fast
gives the illusion of less grandeur
than walking

The sun would surely burn me
My eyes would sting from sweat

Thoughts of my mother in a nursing home
drifted through my mind
Would my knees end up like hers?
Crippled
Dead even

By the time I reached my gate
I turned around and went back to the house
I'll walk another day

conversation

I wish I had a Coke
go to the store
I'm cold
get a blanket
I really need to work out more
take a walk
I'm lonely
call a friend
I feel alone
you are never alone
I just want to be loved
love someone
I'm tired
rest
I can never win
keep playing
I can't
you can
I want

you have
what do I have?
you
me?
yes, you
sigh
you're enough

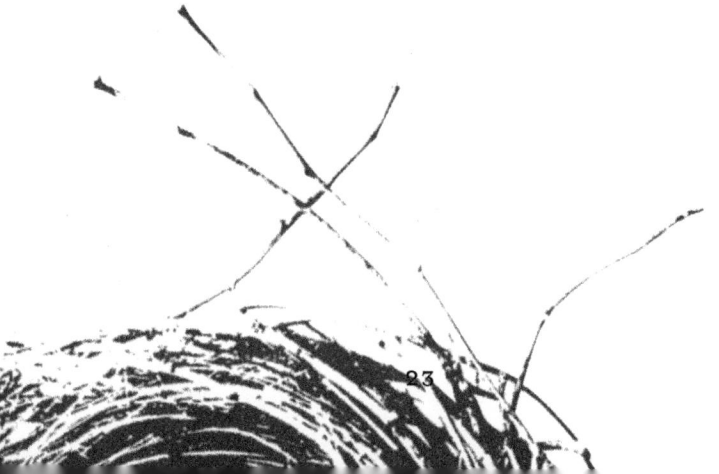

hard to know

when we first met
you were aloof
there was something about
the way your cowboy boots
matched your hair
you always looked the other way
when you drank your beer
playing hard to know

you were waiting on your girlfriend
and it was about to snow
you said she was the funny one
little did I know then
you would be my lover
there was something about your boots and
your hair

though come to find out
it was more about your heart
the one who came to know mine
so hard to know

what she is to me

her fragrance is the salt of the ocean
her taste is the baker's bread
her song is my breath
and I sing her joy
her weeping
her foreverness
in her eyes
I can see
her heart
she sustains my warmth
give me nothing more
than what she is to me

what i've seen

I've seen
angry good men
women sinking in their grief
children, each one defending
what they were born with
I've known smells I could depend on
like hamburgers frying
Saturday nights
like the trains
screaming by our house
they barely let you down
I've seen sacrifice
sickness
longing
I've seen myself in you
I've seen you standing alone
very bad men
women victimized
children destroyed

not to mention joy
a lover's touch
my mother trying to understand
her own death
while living
I've seen my face change
and my age grow younger
a witness to
temporary surcease
legitimate peace
With each day
my eyes escort their knowing
to my soul
I've seen very little
and know little more
but lest this knowing
know no more
I'll see while I can
and be that much more

my places

gather me from the starry night
and bring me to where I am
gather me from the crack I saw when I was ten
I've never forgotten

bring me from my children
without leaving a void
bring me back from my deathbed
let me breathe my last breath now

gather me from the bird in flight
the misshapen clover
faces in the cliff walls
the fragrance of the rose

come to me
all my places
make me who I am
while I live

the muse

(For Billie Holiday)

Billie
Oh my soul
my heart
in my lavender nights
you brought the bluest moon
in the Mayan solstice
you gave me solace
giving the gift
of authentic self

Oh my life
my searching
for the muse
never to end in unsettled sleep
but joy
satisfaction
knowing my best came

and sang
the song only I could sing
Billie
Oh my soul

blood

saddened by separation
nothing consoles me
familiars are lost
leaving roots
only in blood
growing in the same womb
seeing first the same eyes
our common bond has died
devotion is a thin facade
beliefs radically differ
we are strangers in this land
where memories are thin threads
weakened by time
no longer binding
yesterday
to today
the blood indeed
will bind us
and when the blood is gone
nothing more will remain

residually yours

There's little left but only a smear here
No need to explain
I get it
though I prefer a painless death

The pills are a little dramatic, don't you think?
Nice visual, though, to bring it all home
You know me
How about I just walk away
I'll keep the coffin cracked

If ever you should change your mind
ring me
Resurrection never hurt anyone
Meanwhile, and with hazy affection
I'll be residually yours

my megan

We took a walk through the old stones
Do you remember?
You said you knew why the little ones were
there
Baseball players, you said
Beautiful and innocent you were that day
I think about all the times you came running
with awkward bumps and bruises
I remember your smiles
Your smiling eyes held your precious soul
Lying with you until you fell asleep because
your stomach wouldn't let you rest
So much of you still resides with me
My love for you burns as a beacon in my chest
Come now, Meg, and reach through this
ephemeral curtain
Take my hand

Can we try again to be that which should
have been?
My Megan

the line

Yes
we are all connected
I get that
never alone
in my solitude
The village
I abhor those
crossing boundaries
of sacred identity
Breaking and entering
ability sporting arrogance
creates contempt
irreverent and profane
Because you can
gives you no right
Watch me all day long
walking through these fields
sharing breath

on my sunny day
look
just know
this threshold is my own

fit

My closet is full
and every so often
that shirt appears
chartreuse and gold
Thoughts of the dance
the night
you and I laughing
You loved me then
so I wore it
It fit me then
I've not worn it since
Some shirts fit
for a day
Colors fade
seams tighten
and give
as to change their minds
Love inspired me to look
the way you saw me

the mirror of you
Today
my closet reminds me
to wear my soft blue tee

with regard

As life goes
children see
through eyes
of need
Undernourishment
creates lean
athletic
scavengers
Youth combing
streets and alleyways
Feeding
Each one
hungers for delights
uniquely their own
Some grow healthy
Some grow fat
All grow
nourished

under pretense
of *en vogue* ways
Eyes gleam with delicacies
leaving the unquenched
room to grow
Tasting forever, tasting forever
The gut tells
all about
the appetite
of the soul
until
all become
who they are
with regard

ego

This creature that I am
completes me
So much so
Giving me every reason to believe
I am perfect
Each thought
each perception
forms vast allegiances
Considering again
From whence I come
To where I go
To who I am
I am
continually present
correct in my mistakes
given to longings
Divine
Obscene
Gender with gender

Honed to be more
Always perfecting
Never wrong
True to being the one
I am meant to be

half breed

peanut butter and jelly
ebony and ivory
Oreos
my cat
Grandma had a black dad
my hair doesn't match my skin
assholes live forever
that nice guy
raped my sister
hot and cold
hurts either way
like passion
all the time
we are gods
the best and the worst
are possibilities
mix your drink
so a child could taste it
and go unharmed

just as well

I don't give a lot of credence to my birth
nothing more to say
a day when I burst
through the cosmic super highway
Stars all lined up
here I am
super libra
Mom passed out from all my pain
I was sorry about that
tell me something nice then
Feel better
about that pain

She looked at me
a blank stare
Nothing
I was born
in the jungle and raised by wolves

Shit
I want a fairy tale

How about when I rode my first bike?
When you taught me to brush my teeth?
When I didn't want to eat lima beans
they're so disgusting?

The best she could muster
only story I've ever heard
pulling on the hem of her dress
crying
Mommy, I don't like you like this

Dad
flying cast-iron skillets
metal drinking glasses
you had a bad day
Eat your own fist this once

Forget asking why
Forget having any voice at all
we all know it's best not to make Mother
nervous
we all fear making Dad mad
lest we die
and need to get birthed again

There should be a moral to the story
the asshole, I mean
Wolves aren't so bad anyhow
I know how to feed myself
to drink from the rivers
Howling keeps my own beast away
most days

Mom is lined up to get birthed again soon
and Dad is cussing his kids
to hell
In the grand scope of things
it is just as well

used

They say
we create nothing
nor do we ever destroy
anything
Change happens
endlessly spilling
breaking, evaporating, building
crumbs of sameness
discoveries reinvented
Recycled love becoming tragic art
completely unique in the sea
of sameness
Minds filtering refuse
giving life to rubbish
building dreams from nightmares
reinventing what once was
used

with you

Out of the breath of god
I floated
Balanced on a warm zephyr
I landed
Falling onto the bed of you
I sighed
Completely in love
I shivered
This, my countenance
ever holy
Pneuma pulsing in my veins
Dwija
the idea that brought me
With you
I'll stay

loneliness

Loneliness tugged me into her bedroom
sheets, lavender as the night we had that fire
She's a bitch, but you never know it
until she's left you
ensconced in her smoke
I held my breath
long enough to keep her out
yet she came
Soft music pretending to soothe me
lulling me into her furnace
Karen says, "Such a sad affair"
but I know her touch
her skin against mine
nuzzling me awake
My dreams save me each day
long enough
to douse my embers
with wine

Walking now awake and ready
lest she take residence here
inside me
and burn

passionista

Each morning I rise anticipating you
Ritual groove brings me nearer
walking quickly
turning the corner
you are there
Your smile
my gentle sigh
your eyes meet mine
I know you have
what I'm looking for
Each day
you know just what I need
You know me best
somehow
anticipating my challenges
my burn rate
my need to get through
one more day
Never too much

always just enough
your expertise entices me
to return to you
You dare to care
about who you are to me
you let me see all your alchemy
I love you
There, I said it
I love you
my barista

sentinel

Lying next to you
you were reading your new book
not minding my nudges
Dark now
arm over your waist
elixir of your breath
gives me space to float
Your lips press against mine
launching me onto a quiet lake
drifting
Doors open
You're gone now
though staying my sentinel
Such comfort blankets me
keeps me
while death imitates her custody

listen

I turned my head in the afterlife
while ten of your years had passed
It isn't the same here as it is for you
Still, I long for you to listen
Close your eyes for just a year
watch your breathing thoughts
dissipate into the web
just past your vision
I'm sitting here watching you
Would that your heart could touch mine
once more
our essence could fly entwined
laughing from the belly
of our love
hungering no more
Believe me when I say
I am here with you
such a thin veil between us
time playing his game

sleight of hand
Don't believe it
What is real
is what you feel

11/16

Long shadows fall over me
While evening melts over mountain ranges
The east is already dark
The time was called
Recorded
You watch on from the ceiling in disbelief
What had just happened?
Then streams lead to the river
of my tears
My eyes swollen with storms of regret
There is no end to it
Oh my sunshine
how I need you
Knowing you live
how can I rest
If then you knock upon my door
I'll give you my all
unless you require less
You'll ever know just

how much I love you
please then
come
never take my sunshine
away

the color of my eyes

Closing these six doors
turning
I swim
knowing a more certain reality
Voices do not condemn
feelings reveal
sight of a deeper hue of blue
Golden fleck brown ... almost green
in my waking cave never seen
Why do I sedate myself from going there?
Insight
language too sacred for words
nothing is bad here
Eyes perfectly focused
gravity does not apply
flight collides with floating
boundaries are my decision
to go or not
I see my raven dancing with a phoenix, and I

know why
tho' each night
I hold the warm hand of numbness
Brick upon brick
pooling stagnate waters
This heart swirls for release
gushing into knowing
within
the color of my eyes

alone

Turning
I see
no eyes
save my own
People pry
cats stare
love meanders
dogs yearn
This well
drinks of itself
alone
Purging bodily earth
redeeming waters
burst into cool stillness
Slake all who thirst
who dip
who seek
reflection
Drink

and know
your own
alone

messenger

Now it seems
angels come in ball caps and backpacks
I thought when he said
someone told me twice today
I should talk to you
I remembered this is how it happens
that itch of a genetic memory rang a little bell
hanging from a branch of my DNA
Yeah, well, I do a lot of research about
hieroglyphics, he said
I think I am supposed to tell you something
You found it
The gateway, that is
Seriously
This guy just met me
My focus turned to steel
The in-between place is the way in
of course, I knew this

The gateway I've used since first I found it
or it found me
They sent me to tell you
You're not crazy
Then he was gone

now i lay me down to rest

Between the hot and cold of things
simmer
Snow devils dance around
drift
This station watching
impervious to expectation
listening
fighting impulse to influence
judging the sharp edge
Desirous of all
watching the rise and fall of my beloved
I rest

sanctuary

Just yesterday
between my prayer circle
and my circle of prayers
a fallen tree
Such precision its placement
Mother tree stood nearby
Look here, child
between petition and practice
what a cutting divide
Do you see?
Connect your walk and song
Believe in the hawk's flight and the raven's caw
the ocean in these pines
This is your sanctuary

baby boy

Baby boy
Tutu needs you to come on over here
There's sumthin burnin' in ma heart I need you
to hear
That death angel got a grip on you
an' there's only so much your Pa can do
Mama knows there's a light in you
it can't get out 'cause your daddy
the things in him bad true
Tu knows your passion is strong
but baby boy, what you gonna do?
The Man said he'd take you
strip you down and come again make you
Be better than your daddy was, more like your
Pa
Ah baby boy, you gotta be strong
hear dis song
and believe what I done saw
It's your time, it's your rhyme

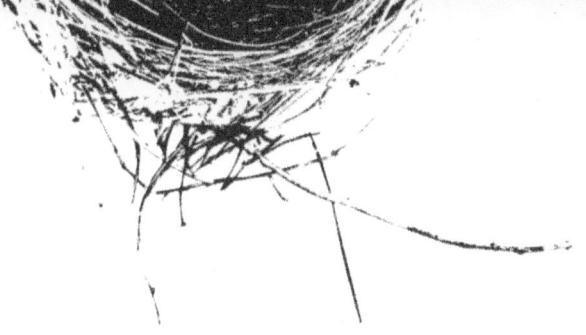

your beat to cheat them death wings
You baby boy, you gotta rise out from da' grip
thems got your head in this trap
and listen'ta me now
or dem wings gonna drag you on out of here
I saw
Ain't no telling when they comin'
What you gonna do
baby boy?

run

This is no ordinary departure
Grave digger dig no more
Swift upon the waters
jumping over the snakes
it's a good race
these vipers are fast as hell
Doris said let's descend into hell one more
time
It's only Hades after all and nothing to fear
Death will come soon for us
But don't stop!
Run!
Young Caleb ran blindly in the jungle
Cliffs taunting his fears
And yet ecstasy and joy were his companions
so then let me find these cohorts on darkness's
path
Little brother, you are my heart

may all I learn be as simple
the grave comes soon
sooner still those who lie down
and fear

sunny

His night crept into my day
as sure as angels sport their wings
his blanket walked into my dreams
Tenderly he choked me
and with ease

Only slightly off from wear
pastels and white
This darkness
What audacity even in the name
to lure
to possess
all the innocence in me

The flicker that remains
sustains

this meandering

Should you wander too far into my heart
It is easy to find your way back
Look for the dark spot
on the other side of the door
from whence you entered
The world abides there
The cars go rushing by
the haze
Artificial eyes watch out
for your mistakes
Blame lurks in the alleys
where self-righteous mud lies under reflective
puddles
The air, riddled with 5G bugs
itching your nerves
urging noonday cocktails
which bring you back to me
This sweet relief
the key in your pocket

warms upon entrance
This expanse
How deep the ocean
beyond orgasmic delight
How much can I bear?
Please don't speak just now
Just be
Your hand
Place it on your heart
Now listen
There in you
I am
and tho' I wish to stop
I cannot
This meandering

communion

What then is this ecstasy?
Divine bliss bringing nothing more unto itself
than itself
Complete Being
The mortal coil
beckons flesh to be the bearer of fulfillment
It is not, and yet we try
Tho' we plead, the answer remains ephemeral
Does the vessel define the experience?
No
such exalted states are reserved
for those whose hearts
are Divine's alone
who want for nothing
Where then is the Divine?
the residence
the yearning
Find her here
at the threshold of longing, she awaits

the lapping wave of desire
she looks at you
and fulfillment complete
forever remains
entwined

this day

Gracious giving
when memories tell a tale
woeful and mournful
Grace prevails giving right where right resides
No matter
Giving thanks in the telling
In the telling all
let us heal
and partake in the truth's felling
to grow anew
this day

ponder

If I had but one chance
how sad to have just begun
Life should tell you
chances are many
growing is forever
but humans ponder lesser things
they innately are
Priests intercede to fill cracks
with old wine
ponder then again
how brilliant is life
how forgiving, charitable
to think we had only one chance
unbearable

aroused

Enchanted
these swirling waters
source unknown
stirring with forces subtle and sure
contemplate creation
Springing from a deep well
this chalice contains elixirs of mystery
molten earth
What is this chaos?
Pierced by creamy white dreams
swirling out of mist
she seduces me
holds me in her arms
claws my ambered heart
only to awaken
in the heat of my desire
left wanting

This day
gracious giving

when memories tell a tale
woeful and mournful
Grace prevails
giving right where right resides
No matter
Giving thanks in the telling
in the telling all
let us heal
and partake in truth's disclosing
to grow anew
cherished and aroused

82

sleep

In my holy place
between breaths
she comes
Her key is true
Others tried, failed
decoys they found
She drives me
I coil around her heat
inside essence
placed on strings
Her melody sings
Haunting glances of other secrets
too deep to tell
too deep to tell
Summoned now
between the veils

queer

2:00AM
the bars used to close then
the plague is here now
and nothing's coming
the asphalt, warm against my cheek
one eye closed
looking down the yellow line
I see
what divides hides
subtler hues
scorn
disdain
mockery
sneering contempt
You never smile
behind eyes awash with beige
gray mud
red leaks between teeth
that streaks to

feet soaked
in a puddle of old, caked brown
someone else's blood
I step away
any other day
my vivid may have puddled
not today
chartreuse, emerald, lapis lazuli, pink
spectrum of this my gem
given
taken by none
there's that line again
you there
me here
pigment
queer

defy

So much water
flows beneath these bridges
long, swinging views
of precipice rock and sky

Graves unmarked
but we know
where the bones are
and stay clear

Tattooed with invisible ink
only we see the sign
the other carries

The torrent current
too dizzy to look down
between you and me
so high
any other might die

Greener grasses

Crystal glasses
Rose-colored horizons
Shine and fragrant elixir
Blood in our veins

I'll meet you there
at your shore
or you mine

Let's defy
And fly

tremble

Tremors in chambers
who has the key?
Dungeons inebriated
Potions that cannot contain
heartache
There is no god
who can rescue
this condition
Time, what time?
Masturbations do not ease
even in momentary heaven
it is not resolved
Mother, please
not again
what I can no longer bear
I bear
left to tremble

pocket

Here in my pocket is your ocean
I feel you swoosh, bubble, and tease my shore
There is no cold, no danger
rather it is warm and comforting
keeping a space of wonder

Sand between toes
laps of salt kiss between us

Ever moving
beautiful
ever still
Still now
Yes, you are

We make the ebb
we make the flow
This ocean in my pocket

grace

You come least expected
My smile is your reward
Most often accompanied
by my lover's touch
How often I need you
But you
no demands stir you
You cherish the moment of your longing
until
you softly land upon this tortured brow
You kiss with tenderest lips mine
Peace
never earned
Given
Grace

wait

It is in the wait
that tests me
Pining consumes
this banquet of trifles
The craving
waters my tongue
and from this table
I see you coming
The wait is the meal
Set me then upon the table
of this yearning
Baste me with your desire
Taste me before I'm gone
Tender longing
slake this thirst
never
As the wait is the all
and nevermore
was it
the feast

air

This air
this sword
it slices these chambers
blood pouring over
misunderstandings
What minds could crash into union?
not ours
too busy questioning
doubting
piercing into accusations
far from faith
What breath shared but, no
this is not that
This is pain, and such could slice the air of
love
to bits and pieces of bloody pulp
leaving conscience to reparation
to regret

Air, mighty and sharp
cut not into the innocence of God
lest what is severed be no more

t or c

Consequences don't knock kindly
they burst through the door
and claim
Smoking
beside the desert brush
begs a flame
so does the water
Then comes the truth
Then comes the shame
Then comes the scar
Jubilee has come and gone
yet Turtle is where redemption lies
These walls tell me you were tortured
even more than our meth-head neighbor
and that's a lot
No one can understand why you are with me
Seems you are showing them all the reasons
why you should go
Why do you stay?

It certainly isn't Sorry Bear
nor is it the plethora of vases
The paintings are nice but really, why?
I have become your consequence
Your Shame
Your Scar
This isn't your truth
or mine

happy

Each morning while
coffee brewed
Ten years
the picture of you
through my window
Chestnut
red mane
curious
about my gaze
I loved seeing you
smelling
touching
your velvet nose
Those apples
How I first won you
And you, me
A perfect pair
Then as if by mistaken magic
You vanished

Oh I know you're fine
I just miss you
Your stature
beautiful
touched me
As things go
things go
people go, too
and so it is
My time may come soon
Who knows how the wind may blow
Fare thee well, old girl
The picture of you remains
The pasture will never be the same

oceans

Turquoise green
Ocean deep
Diving into swell upon swell
She holds me
Wet
Breath
Salt upon my lips
She kisses me to sleep
Upon her breast
Just love me
I cry only one tear
To anchor upon the shore
Of her sighs
Her waves
Her ocean eyes

fire at sea

Adrift my heart
I am nowhere to be found
Hearts strewn behind me
floating away
salt bites my christened skin
oh stingray, go on now
why is the inlet so narrow?
the constant spray
she chokes me
the map smolders
smoke and ashes my sextant
foolishly I stand bow upon the pulpit
erect and still
God is silent
No guardian sweeps over my journey
I am alone in this quandary
to know where my heart belongs
to know and see nothing
no dove

no fig
no horizon
On fire
adrift at sea

blessed

We awake
We are so blessed
We walk
We are so blessed
The children laugh and play
We are so blessed
Still and lifeless our daughter lies
We are so blessed
Death of our children
We are so blessed
Falsely accused
We are so blessed
Ill stricken
We are so blessed
Comforted in our pain
We are so blessed
Hopeful for the rain
We are so blessed
Prophetic visions

We are so blessed
Enslaved, robbed, murdered
We are so blessed
Guns of angry young men
We are so blessed
Genocide
We are so blessed
Lies, manipulations, greed
We are so blessed
Earth
We are so blessed
Family
We are so blessed
Love
We are so blessed
Tell me then the source of these blessings
Tell me now so I may know
Unyielding, without favor
Visited upon the strong and the weak
Given to none and all
We are so blessed

stone

When I was eight
I calcified
Too many trips to the asylum, I guess
Mother, rest her soul, had the blackness
hanging over her
Men and God had taken her and did as they
pleased

Her armor was different than mine
Hers was a veil that dropped, sweeping her
away into the abyss of her demise
She thought it was all her fault—the way those
mens used her up
She just knew God had cursed her
She was right
God wasn't interested in Mother's plight
or in mine

The truth is, Irene was lovely
Heaven knows she's lovely still, and with any
hope, there have been a few apologies said

*God, have you told my sweet mother that you made
a couple of mistakes with her? Have you said those
words she needed so much to hear? Please tell me you've
said you were sorry and asked for her forgiveness*

The truth is my Mom had a heart of gold
pure flawless gold
hers was the sunset in my eyes kind of gold
that showed me her shiny heart
and her Godly hell at the same time
I watched her take that putrid soup in her
sickened soul to an absent God and plead
She lay slain over the songs of David's soul as
she poured into the Psalms
She cried until her tender knees were numb,
red, and swollen

She bled and wailed over the heads of her ten
children, pouring that liquid syrup molten gold
over each one of us. God owed her that much.
Each one she ushered into their old earthly
age, even me when all the odds were against
this rock lasting

The Lord's redemption draweth nigh unto the
ten Apple kids because of Irene

Mother nailed herself to that railroad-tie cross
and then proceeded to carry it

*For the love of all that is righteous and holy, God, you
better be taking care of my mother because, as I live
and breathe, I exist because of Mom's calloused and
bleeding prayers*

Don't you see?
I'm *here* because of Irene, and I am *here* to tell
my story of miraculous redemption
because of the wildly brave and enchanting,
schizophrenic, magical brazenness of madness
she poured over me
So now I am in my madness working my
alchemy
This is me pouring my mother's gold

Mom brought me to the molten pot of
quicksand and said
dive, daughter, dive. No mens are gonna catch you. You

gotta learn to swim in the epizootic of dis world and
do it again and again until those knees grow roots and
God finally turns his head and looks at you

I love you, Mom
I love your crazy-eyed trips with me into hell,
and I love your drug-hazed escape into the veil
I love you turned me into stone and then
kicked me into the bubbling lava pool where I
learned to properly drown
I love you, Mother
I am your daughter
I'm your golden nugget
I am your rock
selah

Love,
Jia

www.ingramcontent.com/pod-product-compliance
Lightning Source LLC
Chambersburg PA
CBHW051321120626
46547CB00015B/2338

9 7 8 1 9 5 7 4 0 8 1 1 8